BETWEEN THE ISLANDS

Born in Cornwall, son of an Estonian wartime refugee, **Philip Gross** has lived in Plymouth, Bristol and South Wales, where he was Professor of Creative Writing at Glamorgan University (USW). His 26th collection, *Between the Islands,* follows ten previous books with Bloodaxe, including *A Bright Acoustic* (2017); *Love Songs of Carbon* (2015), winner of the Roland Mathias Poetry Award and a Poetry Book Society Recommendation; *Deep Field* (2011), a Poetry Book Society Recommendation; *The Water Table* (2009), winner of the T.S. Eliot Prize; and *Changes of Address: Poems 1980-1998* (2001), his selection from earlier books including *The Ice Factory, Cat's Whisker, The Son of the Duke of Nowhere, I.D.* and *The Wasting Game.* Since *The Air Mines of Mistila* (with Sylvia Kantaris, Bloodaxe Books, 1988), he has been a keen collaborator, most recently with artist Valerie Coffin Price on *A Fold in the River* (2015) and with poet Lesley Saunders on *A Part of the Main* (2018). *I Spy Pinhole Eye* (2009), with photographer Simon Denison, won the Wales Book of the Year Award 2010. He won a Cholmondeley Award in 2017.

His poetry for children includes *Manifold Manor, The All-Nite Café* (winner of the Signal Award 1994), *Scratch City* and *Off Road To Everywhere* (winner of the CLPE Award 2011) and the poetry-science collection *Dark Sky Park* (2018).

PHILIP GROSS

Between the Islands

BLOODAXE BOOKS

ISBN: 978 1 78037 506 9

First published 2020 by
Bloodaxe Books Ltd,
Eastburn,
South Park,
Hexham,
Northumberland NE46 1BS.

www.bloodaxebooks.com
For further information about Bloodaxe titles
please visit our website and join our mailing list
or write to the above address for a catalogue.

Supported using public funding by
**ARTS COUNCIL
ENGLAND**

Cover design: Neil Astley & Pamela Robertson-Pearce.

This is a digital reprint of the Bloodaxe 2020 edition.

ACKNOWLEDGEMENTS

Acknowledgements are due to: *Birdbook: Saltwater and Shore*, ed. Kirsten Irving (Sidekick Books, 2016); *The Book of Love and Loss*, ed. R.V. Bailey & June Hall (Belgrave Press, 2014); *The Clearing*; *The Compass*; *Cordite*; *Hwaet! 20 Years of Ledbury Poetry Festival*, ed. Mark Fisher (Bloodaxe Books, 2016); *The Lonely Crowd*; *Magma*; *Manhattan Review*; *Metamorphic: 21st century poets respond to Ovid*, ed. Nessa O'Mahoney & Paul Munden Recent Work Press, 2017); *The North*; *Poetry and Place*, with art work by Dianne Firth (Belconnen Arts Centre, Canberra, 2017); *Poetry Review*; *Sea-Fever: a collaboration*, with Bruno Van Dijck, Mike Perry, Pete Judge & Jeroen Laureyns (De Queeste Art, Watou, Belgium, 2016).

And thanks to: Heather Parnell, for her art work, *Pocket Remains* ('Pyroglyphs'); Jenny Pollak and Luis Vidal, for 'pequeñas cositas de nada' ('The House of Innumerable Things'); Mike Perry, for the *Sea-Fever* collaboration ('Three Fevers and a Fret', 'A Wave') and Pete Judge ('Flugelhorn on a Pembrokeshire Beach').

The epigraph is from *Carnac* by Guillevic, translated by John Montague (Bloodaxe Books, 1999).

CONTENTS

Nous n'avons de rivage, en vérité,
Ni toi, ni moi.

We have no shore, really,
Neither you nor I.

GUILLEVIC, *Carnac*

Edge States

1

Sunlight, late
              in the year, the edge
of winter. Light like stainless steel.
Just out of hearing,
                the ring
of its thin blades fencing with itself.
Light like glass
              that, let fall
on water growing harder at the edge
of freezing,
             could break.
Its splinters on your retina. And the wind
like a slap to the skin,
               the wind
stretched low to the lake, to the bare shore
where you wait
              for light, and tears
the cold brings, all the purer without
tincture of emotion,
               tears to clean
the eyes, for no sake but the sake of clarity,
which should sting.
               This wind,
then, cutting through the dry reeds,
sharpening
              its edges
on the water, *shick-shick* like the slap
of ripples,
              as if on a stone.

2

Closer now. At the edge,
at your feet, a small undercut lip
of first ice, that the ripples seem to slow to

then duck under...
The edge going milky, glaucous,
agate-like. In the splash zone, droplets still

to frosting on the least
grass blade they touch. But the ripples
don't cease. Under the held breath of the ice crust,

something like a pulse...
In melt pools, a trembling up, each
different inflection of the under-rhythm. Lake-breath.

And quieter now (if you
crouch) hear the creak of the ice-skin. A squeal,
like a wince. A click and shift of pressure like a sigh,

the crackling never
where you look. Here's how a fish
might know it, rising from the silt. The way ice speaks.

3

Or say it slow, in small
words. (Friends, this is
for you; at the edge

where the differences
touch, you and me,
state and state,

where Siberian wind
leans down to lap
the level Baltic,

it's all a vowel-shift:
too numb-lipped
for consonants,

the words take shape.)
Simply:
I went

to the lake. Sat
on the stone. Met

wind. And sunlight,
too loud. Finally

it was the least,
the quiet thing, the ice

that spoke to me.

Mänttä, Finland

Erasures

like the dream in which every new
page, in however new-bought-crisp a notebook,

was a jostling concourse of words.
Departures, destinations. He had to greet each

of them, each as itself, before he could begin

the real work: to see them gone –
to start rubbing out one here, then a line

there, then a strip torn, then tatters all over,
to disclose a particular space

with nothing in it but the rise and fall,

the crest, break and eddy, the shape
of particular breath: the timbre of a voice,

hers, his, the print each left in him, that revealed
their absence, or that their absence revealed:

like walking on a thinning shingle spit
to the horizon, with the sea's hush either side.

Nocturne with a View of the Pier
for NC (1951-72)

West Pier: its too too solid ghost:
a frayed draggle of girders
like poorly plucked feathers, dangling,

the accidental poise of archaeopteryx
pressed like a flower in its limestone,

delicate as dancing.

Ghost-contraption with curves
of a 1950s fridge or wireless
– old modernity

called up to haunt us
camply, in a seaside-postcard

Brighton sort of way.

A storm-wrecked ghost train,
bent track and slammed doors
and rattlebone props, cast adrift

in green-grey-opal-veiny sea,
facing a hundred hotels' blank

gaze, no way back to shore.

*

As Stephen Dedalus (young enough to like the pose of old-
    before-his-time) said:... *pier:*
a disappointed bridge. And yet, there's this,

this larkiness that takes us, ice creams dripping in its mitt,
        this sense of music at the pier's
end, even when there isn't. How to understand

these moments when people who don't do that sort of thing
        find themselves walking the boardwalk
straight for the horizon, hand in hand?

*

A pier is a tease. A come-on
                even when it's empty.
It would go too far, it is suggesting, if it could.

*

A pier starts as a simple
story, there and back. But with a hint

of leaving: the stern of a once-upon-a-
liner, casting off, always pulling away,

with that large soft melodious groan
of a hooter as it lets go,

a Bank Holiday lover rolling aside
in the next room, briefly

sated. People at the handrail,
waving – gradually, we realise,

diminishing… and
suddenly not trippers any more

but emigrants. Quick!
Go clattering for the gangplank

(a pier is a grandaddy
of all gangplanks) back to terra

firma. Too late.
You can't get there from here.

*

Does a pier secretly want
to be an island? Or:
does a pier want to be an island,
secretly?
            (Friends, family, couples,
joined by words, may be coming apart
at the commas:
                school-mates
awkward in a shared room, you
and I – yes, you know who you were –
learning the punctuation –
                            small
signs, nothing in themselves,
connoting so much
                    of the space between.)

*

In a parallel world where politics, and war,
                have been replaced by holidays
two nations face each other, bristling
        with interlocking, longer, longer piers:

the strait, like a zip fastener.
                    Day trippers can saunter
pointedly, right past each other
          almost to each other's shore.

*

Always the other one, the lesser, West Pier Minor...
The one famous thing he did was to burn.
To stand up in a body of smoke. Then we turned.

We still talk about him, sporting his new uniform of flame.

*

In Regency Square, there's a bench
that's home to some – four or five
out there today with their carrier bags
that clink, with their flushed faces:

those ghosts of good cheer.
Of gestures: hail-well-met. Again,
again. Of Happy Hour

forever, like an island, slightly offshore
and eroding, and the causeway gone.

*

Something ruffled the folds,
I could swear, of the shallow bay window

three floors up. It's taken me an hour
to walk back forty years.

Friday night with a festival air about it,
arcades rattling, synapse-flashing like a pepped-up brain;

spiced smoke and musics – here's a Regency
quartet, a grizzled Blues band, then a flare

of fado, is it, or flamenco, like a bouquet
thrust in my hands by a stranger... Here's begging,

frankly, and the once-bombed Grand Hotel
up-lit in mauve. Crowds. Here's me, playing flâneur

till I see how far I've gone; it's further
out than I'd remembered, the street smaller,

the house not a guest house any more,
blank... except, three floors up,

what might be shadow folded in the curtain lace
by streetlight, no more certain than the lack

left on wallpaper where some furniture,
I can't say what, had been,

no more sure than this sudden
seeming to remember

that I looked out once, or was it you
who told me? Down on the opposite pavement,

blurred as if not quite adjusted to the focus
of the world you saw, a grey man

looked up. Turned away. Was gone.
You liked a good ghost story. Now

forty years on, look, I'm here.

*

A pier is a nowhere . Shifting sea beneath.
That queasy glimpse.

They leave the gaps between the planks on purpose.

They know that we (really, deep down) want to know.

*

Another, and another round of cold
toast, way past wanting, from my hotel breakfast

as we learned to, then, feeding up
on the one paid-for meal of the day –

and again, like a juddery film clip,
the stuck moment (as a ghost might be,

a self's back-eddy circling itself
till it fades). *I'm sick of it*,

you said to the window one morning.
And I didn't ask. Another round

then, cold. What can I do
with this hunger, that's not mine,

that I can't feed by eating for two?

*

In the bevels of the hotel mirror, slivered lives
peering back at me, some of them mine,
from then: a childhood half demolished,

a me-to-be under construction, me uncertainly
eighteen, a bit of a Dedalus (*Ulysses*
was on the reading list, at least),

me-then, almost as gone as you. No,
more so: overlain by me, me older,
whereas you would be a new

wound always in friends, family
or anybody left to think
That last time we spoke...

If I'd known..? If I'd said...? You,
on the bridge. On an edge
no one saw. Then no you.

Had it come to you then, or had it been weeks,
or years, there'd been this other
crossing you'd had secretly

in mind? We, everyone who'd known you,
talked, talked ourselves into pieces,
but nobody knew.

*

Last busker with his drum kit underneath
the esplanade, with his tish-clash, his gut-
thumping shudder and roll... When he tires,

as he must, as in good jazz there's
                    that moment
                              falling
into step and place and rhythm, where
he's gathered back, the solo, dead beat
now – back and into the pulse, the breath
the waves on shingle, clash
                    and back-sigh,
                              of the theme.
And now the sea-front lengthening in darkness.
Strung tenuous lights. The aged skiffle boys
are still out, with their gleaming scooters.
And the birds, dark shapes, are homing,
                    going one way,
                              there:

*

the West Pier. A cage without bars, as if made
for flocks of (other people's) memories,
their swirls, their murmurations, safe
roost, in the twilight...
                    which might be a name
for exile, or the state-beyond-their-time
of expats; it's their choice: go home,
and be the ageing too-tanned
stranger;
          stay abroad
and be the pale unchanging one,
the true ghost.

The Age of Electricity

Already we're those creatures our grandparents would not recognise – the
children of electric light,
                    of nights on the town, of the thousand bulb
fairground waltzer, waterfalls of neon up which appetite thrashes to mate.

How many of us were conceived not in the tactful dark, but...hey,
leave the light on – born a bit more knowing, just because of that?

Don't you feel it fizzing in your chromosomes, those tweaks of the helix,
filaments of what a darker age called fate?
                    Or see its blips on the cortex,
eyes closed, or blindfold, sparks like static prickling your inside night?

No escape from it now, not even if a sneeze of solar plasma ripped our
grids and stamped the grand marquees of glow above our cities flat;

our bodies won't forget. Age ten, dared to it,
                    I lick-tipped my torch battery
terminals; it's still there, the squirm of small volts on my tongue, fizzle-sweet

like dangerous sherbet. Or, age five, marooned by lights-out: I'd
forgotten how to sleep. At last, my mother took me out to meet

midnight in person. Streetlights clicked, zizzed, off to on, as they saw us,
pavements shivering awake. What
                    kept her walking, the two of us walking,
me almost asleep and still walking, beyond our own or any street

I knew, I couldn't say. I huddled close in the long-ago-mothbally dream
of her beaver-lamb coat

that smelt how forever might smell. It felt right,
                    to be walking, on, on, out to
the ends of ourselves and beyond, out of sight.

Touched

Just like that, in a crowd... A shadow touched him,
     opening his senses, each to each.

He wades into the penumbra, up to his knees
     in its satiny silt. He goes by touch

where it deepens, in the grey of night-sight
     where the light turns granular

against the tongue like halva, sweet and dry,
     or clings to him like cashmere

holding his skin's warmth to his skin. I might
     be half an angel, he thinks, or

whatever those bodies are called that breathe,
     consist of, and who knows, maybe

feed on, light – half and equally, dark. He feels
     the photons prickling like blown spray.

By night he hears the thunder-crush, like surf
     beyond the dunes, of sun. The taste

of it, its salty crystals drying to his contours,
     his dark-matter shape... If we

        had eyes to see, he would be sparkling.

A Wave...

...is what it is. Sometimes, an inquisition
      of the shore. Sometimes a small
retraction, excusing itself. The question

      (and it is a question, each time) is
of what it lifts and what it leaves. Hey, wave,

are you vamping to a rhythm – your almost-
      predictable rise, your sync-
opation at the fall...the way the up-swing

in you tenses, riffles and (just at the teeter-point
      where a surfer might *go*!)

bursts? Is
      flung down. Given up.
            A busted flush.

*

A wave
      is singular and plural. Human pyramid
aquiver
      as it builds – shoulder to shoulder,
hand to hand,
          Picasso's *saltimbanques*
(this is his Blue-
          Green Period) are flexing up
a skinny spangled child
          right to the apex
of the Big Top's gasp and sway
           till they break
in a crash-spring and tumble, to head-over-heels
and bows. Sweat, glitter. To the surf's applause.

*

A wave
      is one pulse of a tide – how each new push
co-operates, nudging the new-stitched edge
of tide-dreck (black weed, foam-scurf
and cuttlebone) up

an inch (with ring-pull, string, polyurethane foam,
the ocean's takeaway that's never
what it ordered quite)
then hesitates:

              and so

                    the impulse ebbs,
               each next wave leaning in
          with less conviction, the weed drying
and popping with sea-lice, sideways, as the gulls

                  drop hop-ambling in,
           the sea-professors with their small
        gold specs, with their podium strut, to stab
at any squirm that might disclose a scuttle. Then

                  it's free for all,
            a conference of cackle
       rubbishing our fine distinctions
     between feed and greed and need.

*

A wave
      leads me astray,
I know, in thinking that it's *one*

or is a thing at all, one that arrives
from somewhere. Wave, I know, though eyes
deceive me, you're just molecules that churn and turn

going nowhere. Stress patterns welling up in us
have crossed whole oceans. We are not
exempted. The kid by the pier, him
in the pirate teeshirt, looking
desperately entertained

and yet somehow marooned – what
do we say: that he, or I, are just our century?
Get off, wave, with your nagging inquisition. We
confess, right? Gather up your tide, as much of us
as you can carry, all the picnic things, and go out, go.

Shag, Rampant

Not a bird but a shaving of black
slivered off from a wave-tip
by a flight path level as a blade,
      he's a wisp,
a twist of lathe swarf, after-
image of the sunlight's flash-
back from the every-angled heave.

Now he's the one still thing
in all the surge-insurgency,
our slim Bonnie Prince Curly
      with his quiff,
his emerald sheen, would-be-
heraldic – just a hint of irony
in his delicate beak. Now he's off

again, hell-bent, kissing the swell
and always at an angle counter
to the way you're going. Or
      he sits
low-wallowed in a trough, spring-
loading himself for that flip up
and dive…gone now for minutes, for

too long, to bob up, too far, where
you (always) weren't expecting,
with a shimmy, to shrug himself dry
      yet glitter –
not the same shag, surely, but as if
the sea had each time re-conceived
the idea of 'shag'. I can't believe

they breed there, in the boulders
among hisses, grunts and wheezings
like a satanic steam machine
    beneath dark cliffs.
No, each shag is a one-off, perky
rag of shadow with its crest up,
question-mark-shaped like a wry

Oh yes? It's the sea's riposte (believe
me, I have its authority to tell you
    lies like this)
to too much daylight, too much
dazzle, too much blue.

Himself

A small bull,
squat and ginger, in a field
under fells – on the tourist route; maybe
that's what leaves him looking vaguely shamed

but still considerable,
a blunt bull, so unmoving
it's a violence almost to the eye: himself
cast in bronze, on the plinth of, commissioned by

whom but himself
while round the moister
corners of the field cows move,
and heifers, slightly, constantly, cropping, at cud.

He's as still
as something that resists
comparison; any likeness, even
to (especially) another bull inflames him; he

might have to kill.
For now, though, he's rapt
in the fact of himself. His bulldom.
It's a poser. Does the lank long dangle of his prong

explain him: the will
rebooting, maybe, the old life-
and-death and for-a-living, chug-chug-
idling libido? He's cornered, in the mid field of his life

that's suddenly an edge,
the rest dropped into precipice,
most of Cumbria with it, into rising mist,
the cough-slip of the scree an echo's length below –

nothing else for it now but to stand
his small ground. Or he's gone
beyond that, saint

of bull-hood, deep
in contemplation.

He could be praying for us.

Firepower

They were bombing the sea.
      I saw this, off Land's End – low
above our hollow hip-hoorays, strike after strike:

Buccaneers, Hunter Harriers, Sea Vixens, (yes,
      I was fifteen, I could name them)
as the broke-back *Torrey Canyon* smeeched

on its reef. The slick spread. Sullen flounces
      and brief flirts of flame, lost
in its smoulder. This was Cnut with high explosives

and Caligula declaring war on Neptune
      and my boyhood; the Atlantic's
great grey shrug towards us, with its downed

and drowning guillemots, already
      washed up, shrunk to burnt
wicks of themselves, the stink of tar,

us cheering feebly, and firepower
      powerless, out of its depth

*

...just as forty years later, slow
      bellies of smoke
dragged off over the hills: the foot-and-mouth
      pyres sluggish. Lost

up a backroad home,
      we glimpsed a lick
of slack flame out across the valley, goaded
      by a line of silhouettes

in armour, their flamethrowers
          poked like cattle prods.
Trucks (khaki) with tarpaulined payloads
                    (grey) thumped up the lane;

as we slewed to the verge. *Don't
     look*, we told the children,
then we couldn't, could we,
                    tear our gaze away?

*

The usual nee-naw, off
to some kids' mischief –

big rubbery gouts of smoulder,
the consummation of tyres

in the old bugger's yard
like his lifetime of grudge.

It was a Guy Fawkes hoard
that saw no reason, in these easy-

credit days, to wait. The shock
was over in a breath's length

but still, a crack in the surface of things,
through which it made sense:

how fire could grapple up a city
by the armful, into swags of smoke.

The slowness. How before
we thought of running we might stop and stare.

Pyroglyphs

Beyond the softnesses of squirrel, sable,
the more liquidly flickering kinds

of weasel, there is mouse-whisker,
down-feather of cloud-pheasant, newborn baby's hair.

Don't credit the word 'air brush'. There is nothing
to be said with that in your calligraphy.

But look into the fire.

Pick one flame. Watch how it licks
itself, its frayed point, to the finest

definition. Try to read,
then to write, what is sketched by that tip.

In the lost script of the silent people,
thirty-one characters seem to refer
to shades of being
absent – e.g.

'the sense that someone has just left a room
where they were never present' or
'the state of having left what
is no longer there'.

There is a possibility
that you will understand them.
You have been warned.
Do you want to read on?

Among the rakings out of last night's bonfire,
this: a flicker book of stills,

charred to negatives, each brief exposure
of maybe an almost a face as it twisted away

but not before its glance burned in
as her or his face turned away might scorch the other

to the heart. Here's a snap of the heart,

its heat-print on the moment, here's its ash-print
on the air. They'll keep the albums, the two

matching albums of each other, see each other's faces
riffled by in all the windows of a passing train.

As if the most mundane
and crumpled of us might reveal
in the body one day
what the mind hardly dared

suppose: spontaneous
combustion – every cell
resolving, in a kind of Rapture,
God's equation, e = mc²

With a lighter-than-thinking brush-point,
a less-than-a-finger-tip's flick, in an eye's-blink,

a kiss to the page: a mark left without pigment
or ink – the almost weightless imprint

in the grass, the pad-scuff in sand
where life brushed past us, so close: signs

the old bush people knew. Ten thousand years

they shared the land with wildfire
in its season. Untended now, it stalks

the gardens of the suburbs, leaving crude
graffiti we can't read beside our looted bins.

> *Where the angel of fire passed over*
> *and did not stop*
> *to knock:*
> *a darkening...*
>
> *Where it came low, slowed*
> *and let its wingtip brush*
> *between the streetlight and the blinds:*
> *its shadow, with us...*
>
> *Where it hesitated on the gable:*
> *soot-fall*
> *in the bricked-in chimney,*
> *its grit on the page...*
>
> *In the morning a scar, a charred*
> *hole burned clean through*
> *where it entered: as close*
> *as we'll come*
>
> *to beholding the face,*
> *to transcribing the one*
> *and unsayable*
> *name.*

Three Fevers and a Fret

(after John Masefield, 'Sea-Fever')

sea   sleepless   (*how can sea*
                sleep?)   fever-fretted
in its oily night sweats
(*down   you must go down to me*)

sea-tossed and tide-wracked   (*listen*
             lay your head down close
enough to hear   my tiffs of wind
my short-breathed shingle hiss)

all night   the dark behind my eye
             blooms dimly   spray-mist
falls back   leaving   whose is this

tangle of filaments   frayed and knotting
             nerve ends in the weed   whose
                   is this inconsolable gull cry?

*

Five a.m. and they're yakking and yowling, the sea's
             appetite unhinged. Just yesterday
one rapped on my window with that crazed
eye, that skewed side-stare straight at me,

big stroppy black-back with his slash
             and jab at anything, his neighbour's
chicks, our stinking binbag, who cares.
Some alarm: it's fight and flight now, smash

and grab at the sky: the sea's hunger astray
for a raid on the landfill at the dumptruck's heels,

hunger that grows with feeding, never
filled
        but wakes us with its clangour
at the tideline of our sleep, and whether
it's the sea's or ours, this hunger, who's to say?

*

*Strange freight you give me − neither dead
nor living. Nothing in its molecules
will melt to my embrace. Is this what you
meant with your myths of ever-after: never*

*rotting, never rusting? Even iron
grows to trust me in the end. Release
me, it says. Shell, bone…Even glass
returns to sand. So we sift down.*

*Nothing should float for long. Things need to rest.
But this…?*
            *In gullet, gizzard or the gut
of me, I who know everything by touch
can't reach it, alone in its terrible dream: to be blown
and driven,*
            circle in an eddy,
                        last
beyond endurance,
            never find a home.

*

*I am sick, sea says. You must listen. Sick
of many things, including your pathetic
fallacies. That song you thought you heard
wasn't mine… At last night's bins in the deserted*

market, listen; the snatch-mobs of dawn
are at those innards spilled as if your own,
the day's trick. And the tall ships stitching
trade routes round the earth, to bag, to cash
and carry...
           Listen. Catch the glitter-swish
of shoals switching grey-silver-grey to
off. The shiver-to-stillness of the coral
bleaching. The slow spreading of the spill
to pools of silence. The hundred-mile spool
of whale song snapped. I have no words for you.

Equator

Rimbaud: the last photograph

Dark snow falling, snow in Africa
and through it, this horizon, this equator,

this crease, fold or fault-line
in a bleached-out photograph or

life...I am already half a memory,

the image of an image, sun-
blotched, damp-stained, falling

between distances, alone,
poised, paused, like a wish, like a

what? You lose sight of me

here, on the lip of the known
world, down the crack between

the future that I lusted for
and what will be

the past. Yes, I could be at home

in these shadows and rumours,
with fever-trees, blinding cracks

of sunlight, with bird-shrieks
and river mist rising. So we cross

the line. Into the dark we go.

Southern Cross

Upended, again. And who knows,
we might all be a different way up from now on.
      Twenty hours in the air
are enough to flip the star map on its spindle.

Constellations I don't have a name for
facing away, circling the south, in a different dance...
      They stopped me, seen
between the branches of the eucalypts self-stripped

for winter, lovely bark hanging off them in shreds,
and the sky, too, in bits. I thought, *I don't know*
      them. They don't know me,
and stood naming them, trying to: Southern Cross

somewhere, for sure... Alpha and Beta
Centauri... as if I were calling them in from the dark
      into the house of language.
How will we set ourselves upright again

having strayed to the edge – so close, a few
      steps through a gloaming
lit more by the white of the bare trunks
than the moon, a few steps to the, yes,

just hand-railed brink, and...? What dropped
      at our feet was the world.
We'd been driving all day, up, imperceptibly
up towards mountains that never disclosed

until now... A thousand foot fall, sheer
       slabs of sandstone still
not dark as if the sun was in them, to the folds
of forest, grey-green fold and ebb and swell

around, somewhere, the inscrutable
       small purpose, no purpose
of ours, of the river in time. There's no way
down, or no way down and back, from here

any more than, next day, us, alone
on the Tableland's bare buckled crust, scarred
       gently by stone axes stroked
to sharpness in the same grooves, again and

a thousand years on...us, looking back,
out, eighty miles to where, lodged in the skin
       of the horizon was this splinter
or tick bite: Sydney. Our world. And again,

where we sat by a slow creek trickling
slower to a pause, hung moment, last
       word, on the canyon's lip
(those flat-earth maps were only half wrong;

there are edges anywhere, just a heart's
trip and stumble away) where it fell, fell still
       unbraiding in its falling
to mist, until gravity lost it; it never hit ground.

Blue Mountains, New South Wales

The House of Innumerable Things
'pequeñas cositas de nada'

...as if the ocean, sidling home around the point,
back from beyond, chose this tide line to present
its findings: crab claw, wisp of fish bone, things
discharged from duty, let go to be...what? Small
points of presence lighting up all corners of the house,
a carnival of detail, a quiet riot. It's nothing

like clutter; clutter is the outward form of nothing
rightly known, a rife amnesia that's lost the point
of itself. But to open the doors, to give things house
room in your true attention, in the present
tense, now, that's a bright recuperation. Small
comfort, you might say, against the slippage of things

into forgetting, but still... The Ten Thousand Things
move like flickers of light across the surface of the Nothing
that's anything but. We dredge in deep-sea sludge for small
and smaller lives – as if a single cell might be the point
of entry into...everything: the birthday present
evolution left, gold-gift-wrapped, on the steps of the house,

unsigned, sure, but surely for us – or else why have a house
at all, why not walk red deserts, bringing no more things
than you can carry on a song? Why not? But this is the present;
no roads on our maps lead back to there. There's nothing
doing at the roadside but a gas pump and some signs that point
elsewhere. The wide horizon's a shut door...till a small

taut *whack-twang*! – like a shot bolt, like lightning writ small:
the whip-bird's Zen slap... And it's open house
to the sky. Child's finger or microscope point
to the brilliance, the multiplicity of least things,
constellations, old footfall of light or, almost nothing
but a refraction on a membrane to show they are present,

the soft stars of radiolaria, drifting, a present-
iment of everlasting. Huge is dumb. It's the small
that whispers the fine information...which is nothing,
as stars are, in the glare of street lights. Let the house
be dark; on shelves, in heaps, the crisp specific things
wait for us down perspective's lane, at the vanishing point

of now...at last, present, as guests in the house
of innumerable instances, the *small things*
of nothing which may be everything, the whole point.

Canberra Rising

That basketball trick: to spin the globe
on a fingertip
                    against the black
of space... So Google-pitch
it to me, reel me in

to when? It could be long enough ago
that it, that blur,
                    that speck
revealed mostly by its shadow
in its other morning

on a street ten thousand miles from here
could possibly,
                    could passingly,
could nine months past,
be me

in a suburb that's mapped by the stars,
a suburb in a family
                    of suburbs
cast over a hillside like a loose-
coiled net,

made of old names, *Wayal, Chuculba,*
and, *Fornax, Antares,*
                    new. Where else
to turn once we'd exhausted the colonially
good and great

but to the sky? The dark. The twinkling out
of languages
                    that vanish when we look

(yet always in the corner of our eye,
whispers of light.)

For days, for weeks, the place was hiding
from me in plain sight,
                              the rational capital
whose logic was that it was neither
here nor there,

something in transit, like a circus tent
slung between tips:
                              the mere idea
of a spire on the parliament building,
the Telstra tower,

the red-eye night-light on Mt Ainslie.
We could wake to find it
                              hauled down
leaving nothing but a bare patch,
some lines of desire,

Lake Burley Griffin drained. Even with blue
sky on it, and civility,
                              the lake that's here
seems less real than the one that isn't:
Weerawa,

Lake George, in its rousing and sleeping,
its dreaming itself
                              back up, or under,
out of nowhere we can track it.
On a shore

shrunk to a notion, it left boats like toys,

a thwarted jetty
        and a paddle steamer,
ghosts of cruises nobody
would wave from anymore.

My last night, and we climbed through close
twists of eucalypts
        our headlights
wove closer, up into the mountain
that had paced

around the city, waiting for me at the end
of every street, until...
        yes: Canberra,
the fallen constellation, at our feet... As if
only as the place

forgot itself, by night, great symmetries
could rise like groundwater
        from a time before
streetlight, or time. As if we could remember:
we slept naked

once, next to the nakedness of space.

The Day of the Things

The day came, as it had to, when the things
reclaimed themselves. An empty room,
open-plan, glimpsed from the train,
one table at a slant

as if a shaft of light had placed it... All the years
we'd been drawing them out, into
ourselves, as dreams, goods,
meanings, wants,

reversed. In the backwash, at first, we fell mute:
daily Dave, beside me at his tablet
on the 8:15, stone-motionless,
the screen blank

and his mirror image pixelating, fading in.
Then he was nothing but his headphones.
Children, they went lightly.
By their bunks,

a games console with gravitas, Lego
like Stonehenge, the parents' panic
from mobile to mobile an on-
vibrate quiver and moan

like wood doves... I could only be glad
for next-door Reg when his Bentley,
waxed bright as a conker,
came into its own.

Doors sighed. Chill atria became cathedrals.
An empty carafe stood amply in
for a whole committee.
But how to decide

now which, was it that Le Creuset tureen
I'd married or that flick of her brush
or her glasses or... everything?
And what could I

be, still here, but the rough-scuffed notebook
I never owned wholly, with this seeping
in, this wilderment of ink,
this tanglewood

of word, root, tendril, from which why
would I wish to emerge, my-
self again and lonely,
even if I could?

The Floes

The floes are breaking up now. Some nights,

thinking back, she sees a blue-black slightly
glowing hulk: that year, another, and the space

between them like dark sky beneath the surface
heaving, clouding when foam flushes over

while on some chilly fragment, as if sat for ever
on the naughty step, or in her impenetrable

own game, the child of her waits; and will
wait for as long as it takes, until the dark gap

between it all narrows again; something stops
this sliding apart of the galaxies, the starlight

thinning, floes like further houses, their late
windows switched out one by one, once recognised

names like bird cries heard from far off, over ice.

Restoration

The restoration room smells high
as a church with woozy solvents:
the cricket-bat smell of linseed oil
or the wickeder stinks
                      I used as a boy
(a killing jar, a whiff of Dabitoff) to fix
the skittery glints of butterflies, for
good, for my collection.

     See them raising the dead, the quiet
     conservators, with their polymer gels,
     their aqueous solutions, micro-fine
     abrasives, dabs of spit
                  on a cotton bud
     (our own enzymes at work digesting
     history), their scalpels peeling single-
     cell layers like skin.

What adheres: dust, the ambient drift
of particulates, smogs, spores, our bodily
fluids carried on the breath, the flakes
of us co-mingling,
                      more promiscuous
than we allow for. And then, the deeper
darkening of paint, from long acquaintance
with the light and air.

     Who wouldn't feel a little like a shadow
     of themselves, clipped by the headlights
     of a coming century, or want such faithful

attendants, these cosmetic
                           surgeons,
savers of the face of paint – to peel you
back to the raw self, the first blinking
brightness? As you were.

As if we were only ourselves at the start... Here
are the marks you made, restored – so literally
the same in times so changed around them
that are they the same?
                           Or there's your then-self
standing out beyond the canvas like a twin
planet right behind the sun, known only
as a tremble in our gravity,

and which is you? Wing-flitters,
dust on the glass, the X-ray plate:
the ghosts of *pentimenti*. In the back row
of the christening photo,
                           a face
out of focus, a family face in costume
of another time. Blink, look again.
Good as new,

the pristine painting (isn't that
what we wanted?) while behind you,
in suspension, in the corner of the eye
or room, as if
                           on a picture plane
of no dimensions, hang what's lost,
what's gained: smirch, scuff and barely
mended scar,

the patina, the palpable erosions
we are known by, plate-tectonics
of a picture-skin that's lived in,
craquelure

       (the one mark forgery
can't fake) that speak for us, for how
we were with things. The work
we do. The work we are.

Bay Laurel

(after Ovid)

Of course I made way for her; I had no choice.
The gust of that girl's panic
                              like a rush of wind
entered deep in the stuff of my cells.
                                        His rage

too like withering sun-glare (he calls it desire)
came crowding in after it
                          into the space
I was. I was spacious
                      not empty. I was everything

that earth and weather made of me: the high
green halls, the slow
                      dark conversations
with the light, the inwardness
                                invaded by...

you call it meaning. I say noise. Trimmed,
pinched to taste, that's my husk
                                repossessed;
myself, evicted
                into nothing you can place.

(That smell...) It is always an exchange:
for every nymph gone to a tree
                              a tree-
soul comes to, walking,
                        struggling to pass

in the crowd, still with her old shade in her,

with her thirst for transpiration,
                                sap
cooler than blood.
                You catch her eye

by accident; it opens in you for a moment,
between you
                and the moment: laurel
silence, the fruit of the tree
                                of unknowing;

you're lost to yourself, lost for words.

A Kind of Rapture

In that moment, all the pages, every one,
the books, scrolls, parchments, all the screens,
the smallest data-nibble on our mobile phones,

fell blank. They stared back empty at us,
worldwide, all at once, like a new revelation.

As if air had been sucked from our lungs.
For that moment, even before panic or dismay,
we all had that blankness inside. As if the sun

in a casual pulse, in a riptide of particle wind,
had wiped us all. That much we'd half expected

but the books... That was the great betrayal.
Now, amongst us, the great hesitation. For some,
the lost faith. But for others, one by one

like the disciples in the garden, at the gutted
tomb, or footsore on the road, it came to us:

the stories, and the poems, they weren't gone
but risen; they were all around us, in the air,
the life of things; we would glimpse them again

now and then, not out of this world but in it
where they came from (like us), where

(like us) they would return, and belonged.

Sea Koan

la mer toujours recommencée...

PAUL VALÉRY,
Le cimetière marin

'the sea begins' – a *koan*
whose inner spaces
centuries of meditation could not fill

in the orchestra pit
of the world's darkened
hall – before sun-up, the sound of waves

or this: coming to sense
an audience
has been there all night in the stalls

through the beach chalet's papery walls
at first light – 'the sea
is getting up' before him

arriving at no time last night
he had been nowhere –
now time itself is washed in on the tide

not sure yet if his eyes are open –
lines of wavering white,
inventing distance, in the northern dim

at some point in the outdoor
        festival (the sea recalls)
the vast drum solo; everyone else walks off stage

                        .

                    'the sea continues' – what
                    more to say? it goes on
                of course, of course, *d'accord, encore*

as in: *la mer toujours re-*
        commencée – for as long
as it scans, and I can see to that

                        but how to read 'the sea
                    concludes'? maybe:
            it rests its case, m'lud – unarguable, surely

'the sea ends': music that builds up
        into a silence
as wave by wave it always tried to do

                    imagine this, on a flotsam
                    spar, washed up,
                these words: 'the sea is over'

How He Lay

Today, for the first time, he lay
   rather faintly, receiving the weight
     of the sun, a not unwelcome burden,
like an extra blanket, like the cat
   that someone he loves, loves. He lay
     like the old, in skin-to-skin transfusion
with the sunlight, to top up the charge
   they can't hold. He lay as if Copernicus
     had not yet spoken; all the spheres
still ground around this axis, audibly. He lay
   the way some sun-besotted leisure-
     takers lie, to secure a strip of the beach
each the size of a grave plot, to work it
   like a medieval peasant, side by side
     not looking up through centuries. He lay
like the Middle Ages. He lay with the sound
   of the traffic (somewhere there was a rush hour)
     or the tide, as if its whisper-depradations
lapped at any summer afternoon, however far
   inland, as if the continental shelf itself
     was sagging, tipping outmost islands
to the edge…like the edge where he caught
   himself thinking, thinking in the body
     not the head, that he lived, as he lay,
alongside granny gravity, their two old
   bodies snug in their familiar knowing. So
     he lay. Then got up. It was half past three.

Flugelhorn on a Pembrokeshire Beach

A sea horn, a silvery
        beach horn cast ashore
on the grey shale, its silvery glint in the sun
against shingle that looks like another weather,
always a later time of day, sadder month of the year.

A horn washed up:
        now, *that* I could credit,
a horn like a conch or a cowrie, picked up
from some layby back along the Gulf Stream. Horn
like a nautilus that's been sailing since…prehistory.

But this was horn
        erect, horn upright,
just above the tideline, and preening its glitter,
its visible flash of surprise: what land is this? Ear
to the ground now, wondering: Could I take root?

Horn, drawn back
        to the waves' edge
now the tide's retreating, as the border collie
with us has to dance and dart back from its herding
of those never quite compliant flocks of foam.

What horn
        says there, at the tide-lip
where the long grey backwash makes a wind-chime
tinkle out of flipped stones, well…though it's just
in earshot, it's not for our ears, not for us to say.

By evening, horn
        had found the cliff path.
Sunset was rigorous and minimal, a single
calibrated line of pink. Horn waited,
I think, and then measured his first note by it.

When horn
            escaped from his own dimensions
he went running out along the steep slabs of the cove
like a race-track's camber, right to the point, the last rock,
flushing the seabirds off their roosts on the way.

    Those dark heads
            surfacing, a hundred feet down,
they were only the rocks the waves heaved back
and over. Not seals hauled in to listen, or to sing.
For rocks to rise and listen, though, that's stranger still.

    When I was young
            there were fog horns
I remember, all down the coast – a lost herd of them
out in the sea-fret. Their call, one to the other (I believe
they are nearly extinct now) was *Come home, come home.*

    In horn's morning
            he's back on the beach,
another, trimmer horn beside, a different glint
of their silvery chrome, their tubes and valves in parallel.
Walk on by. There will be music. Maybe, harmony.

Dear Barber

(for Z)

My head in your hands
for a trim... Electric

razor frisson, a ripple of wind

in the grass, now a stumble of footfall
in the subsoil of the skin,

a jolt through to the bone

and I know what you're holding
circumspectly, as you do

all my flinches and whims:

a brain box? More like stock pot,
Marmite, snug tureen,

its near to liquid slop

(slow cooking, this)
and bubble, scraps and dim

infusions: a life

a stray clot, a slight
spillage could stop. You

steady it – keep

still, this way a little, don't
talk now –

between your fingertips.

Of the Silence at the Heart of Pyrotechnics

You need the dark
to help erect it, that shuddering
vault, that momentary
cathedral built of nothing
but its burning down, its falling angels

cast into the arms
of themselves, their own reflections in the sea.

You need our hush,
our breath-held gulp at the thud
that sends a half-notional
sputter-trail jiggling up
beyond itself. We've lost it. Then the smack

like God's own slap,
that inside-outs the night – splits time

from space, like slate
clean down its line of cleavage. You need that crack
to glimpse the world
as fossil – archaeopteryx
with its wings spread for flight, and further,

its fragments flying out
for ever, yet held motionless: the silence

hidden in the absolute
percussion, the aaah! punched out of us,
our life's-breath scattering.
We're blown apart, and so
together, for as long as it takes one last spark

to pick its way, sore-kneed,
down the gravity staircase. So to bed. So good night.

Between the Islands

Beyond the outer rocks, the open sea...
Event horizon. Foam-fringe like a white
stain on clean darkness. The delivery
of weather rumbles on into the night.

Big wind, that leans too close, testing the seams
of the house, which whimpers. Wordlessness: is this
the point? It tucks us in. Sweet dreams.
Or it bends closer, the enormous kiss

of an Atlantic low, its heavy skirts curled
round us. Starfish on the window ledge,
from strangers' holidays. Where in the world
are we? Or out of it? We're on the edge

more often than we think. Then one of us
is nowhere. Sorry, just to write the word
                    'us' feels presumptuous.

*

Too in love with the new, with the half-absurd
costume jewellery of the rare (a bronze-green-blue-
bee-eater, a solitary storm-foundered bird
half an ocean from home), the twitchers too

migrate, beyond sense. There is more than sense
at stake. This is a stake-out, with the clink of kit,
the lenses taking aim, text wavelengths tense
for dawn. Yes! the twitterfeed thrills to it:

in silhouette, a wind-stretched thorn bush
and look: little beauty. Ticked. So happen-
stance can be possessed. And lost. A stray flash
from a windscreen: it stings like a slap;

the bird's off, flushed into the statistically
unlikely distance, from this one chance
                landfall, back out to sea.

*

You can't trust islands. Nor the circumstance
that's part, that's a third partner, in a friend-
ship. How it shifts. Steepholm and Flatholm dance
slow, do-si-do, out in mid-channel; it depends

which shore you look from. Now, blunt but exact,
a blocky container ship slits through the old
illusion; closeness may be less a fact than artefact
of distance. A foreshortening. Laws of optics hold

our disbelief suspended, the way estuary silt
never rests, the way a multi-storey's-worth
of cars can float, an almost-island built
upon currency flows. As if somewhere on earth

all of our times are places, still there one day
to go back to. One day. When there's time.
                    And look, we're just a step away.

*

The dream persists, that fond beach-bum-Sublime
– the desert island, a blank sheet: ah, to rewrite
the stories selves are...See him, with his sub-prime
mortgage on the land, the castaway, too white

for this sun, and day by day more naked, however
he's patched his rags, plaited the creepers, tried
everything before the first blunt and unclever
butchery for a rank uncured hide.

But grant him his moment, howling at the sea's
edge, running, singing at the surf, Crusoe
to Caruso in sixty seconds, drunk on the release
of seeing, as if on a horizon, the truth: no

sail coming, ever. He's mastered the trick
of scratching his shadow, the first selfie, in the sand.
Waits for the tide's slow click.

*

Sometimes it's lads on a lark, a prank, a grand
night out after the pubs close, a dozen or so
a year daring each other on, on and
over the narrowing spit. Sometimes it's one alone

already out of sight and earshot. It's a mood
of the tides, that fold in both ways, round
this sometime island. If they were arms, who'd
spurn their embrace now, at the laying down

of sunlight, moonlight starting, and the cross-
patterned mesh of their ripples is lacework, the ghost
of a christening robe. Is interference, lost
reception, crackling of light. Is almost.

Is a pulse, is the bleep of Speak After The Tone.
Is after midnight. Is the longer bleep before
                    the disconnect. Come home.

*

I post this, open, unaddressed – 'for
you', a you-shape in the grainy light
of words, along the tideline between *shore*
and *sure*. These shifting breaths. I have no right

to anybody's story, you'd remind
me, with that edge of courtesy
almost as sharp as reproof. Not unkind.
What's between I-and-I is neither you nor me

but wide Atlantic light – the Isles of the Blessed
so close, some days, you could call over…next day
gone, dissolved back into story, as if *West*
was a term for return, grave mounds marking the way

they came, first landfall…folded into mist, like you
inside the wave, then clear horizon, with a tact
you'd recognise. I know you do.

*

A sentimental error, this, to see islands as fact,
the sea as absence ('unplumb'd, salt, estranging').
No, the sea's the living thing. It's the act
of itself – islands, the accidents of changing

tides. One ruck of the bedrock has a crust
of humus, blown or bird-shat seeds, decay making,
remaking itself. It has rains, time and us.
Another's just lodging enough among the breaking

spray for the continual shriek and wheel
of seabirds. Another, no more than a snag in the swell
where it goes crimped or glassy to reveal/conceal
the reef. We can give it a name, a light, a bell:

The Wolf, The Manacles. Nothing of us lives there
but words. As if a word could fix things, friends,
                    adrift. The sea won't care.

*

Land-islands, like their own astonishments
in the mist lake of the Levels. They're beside
themselves, like the perfectly useless remembrance
of the old, a beach suddenly vacated by the tide

before the tsunami. Brent Knoll is a square-
shouldered hunch, Glastonbury sharp and fey
as a sea-mirage, Fata Morgana, nowhere
we can hope to be. The submerged motorway

is traced by two strict shoals of glow, the red,
the white. The past, the future. Athelney's
an Isle again, as when the news-drones overhead
showed miles of flood-scape. A line of trees

wades ashore. Chafed by long drainage, the field
striped with rhynes waits, the Summerland waits,
                    for the sea to return, to be healed.

*

A colony of nowhere that the sea creates
so close to home: they'd see the smoke, the docks,
they can't reach, for weeks, as they unload their freights
of illness here – the cholera, the pox –

to sweat them out. If not, there's soil enough.
Wind scrubs the fever house, if not clean,
at least raw. When the sea cuts up rough
this could be Cape Horn. The kingdom of Quarantine

is a republic now, whose sole commodity
is distance; there will always be a trade.
And now here's Marconi to girdle the earth, three
miles the first step for the first words relayed

over water: *Are you ready... Can you hear
me.* This, slowly, in stuttering Morse. The pause
before *Yes. Loud and clear.*

*

The edge of things. Grey swell, imploding, draws
curtains of spray, draws and tears them; white
on white, some tatters sheer off – gulls. Because
all this is silent, from this distance, now, I write

this litany: Hanjague, Menavaur,
Ganninick, Crebawathan, Rosevean, Gorregan,
Mincarlo – language further out from shore
than Cornish, more like seal speech, a translation

of the same-and-changing sea shapes, now
shags measuring their wingbeats to the dips
of waves they skim, the whirr of puffins, how
terns pin themselves, still almost, by their wingtips

to the sky. Can I who (you would smile) pretend
I 'don't do ritual' share this, the great calm
                    surge, land-and-language's end?

*

The garden, suddenly alight with...you have to say *charm*,
goldfinches mobbing the feed and each other, a blur
of bickering and yellow, a thrill of small alarm
bells jangling each other. Now, as you were.

They're still, intent with purpose. What they know
they know together, as the space around,
between them. They're an archipelago
lapped now by safety; now, a snag of sound

explodes them like a breaker gone for bust.
Strewn, shattered into flight...just as suddenly
recuperated in a hurtling swerve, on the gust
of their shared self. A kind of poetry,

those lines of force that link us, the unsaid
inside the said, the distance that connects,
                    yes, the quick and the dead.

*

White sailboat heading, in the last effects
of light, for the sea lock, blue shading to grey
as the cliff's shadow spreads. It inflects
things into elegy, stealing them away

from themselves. This is an act of piracy.
Let go. Holding the pen gives me no right
to legislate. Let 'you' be who it needs to be.
If 'heading homewards before night-

fall' comes to hand, too timely, as a sign
for dying, the tide tables are its text, no
other book. No metaphor, not mine,
not even yours. When you were readying to go

I had to *read* it, in the paper. It was news
to me. It's that (believe me, I am talking to
                    myself) I find hard to excuse.

*

The ice road is open. This is what they do
on trust, dim haloed car lights following
each other, not too close or distant, through
months-long white dusk, flurries swallowing

their tracks. Beneath its frozen crust, the almost
tideless Baltic, scarcely salt... On a shore
without a foreshore, boulders wait, lost
children of the ice sheet. This is more

like tact, like friendship, than like 'love', that
word that wants to conquer worlds. Here we
can meet, between islands so wide and flat
they're like horizon inked in. Here, the clarity

of cool North light. Nights, longer. Loss
and gain. They listen for the news: *the ice
road is open*. We can cross.

*

Bare jagged skelligs: men clamped in the vice
of the sea, held to the workbench of the soul,
prayed, starved, as if only what did not suffice
flesh and blood was enough. To live at the pole

of inaccessibility, they were breaking
the waves, of the sea, of the self – the mind
as ruthless as the swirl of gannets, one flaking
off, crack, into the surf, eyes open. (They go blind.)

Even here, in our mild wildered churchyard, faint
echoes: some lives lost at sea, some not,
lie under small crags, reef-tips, anchor and chain
and forms of words. Form speaks. It's what

these odd snagged sonnets do – suspend
a rhyme, unfinished business. This is not yet,
                    not and never quite, the end.

*

A postcard from the plains of Dogger, wet-
lands glittering with marsh pools, as the cold
in the bones of the earth relents. Don't forget
the tracks, follow the beasts, between old

inlets easing, intricating into wider
creeks. All of our lives the change had seemed
like seepage. Then one night, the gush: the tide
comes in for ever – what's left, a world dreamed

like this from friends, bright moments and, between,
brief crossings. Here, uneasy winks of light
mark channels. You would know what I mean
by addressing an absence (lend me yours) to write

as if to someone, as if something might respond
beyond the words, the outer rocks, the open sea.
Beyond that...just *beyond*.

Towards a Line from Guillevic

...joy, whether the sea is grey
or a decayed blue.

GUILLEVIC,
Les Rocs VI (tr. Teo Savory)

Far out, something gives, rips, opening a shred of...could joy
be the word? in the overcast: white! and who cares whether
it's feathering back and blown away: the wave, not *a* but *the*
wave, one and only, slow exploding moment where the sea

trips on the last black rock, off the point, and briefly is
no thing except its falling back, folding back into grey
over-/under-cast...lit, for now, as if a lighthouse beam or

inspiration lifted it, coiled dumbness sprung towards a
yes, word you could clutch at, yes, shattered, yes, decayed

but yours. And now the sky concedes a glimpse of blue.

CPSIA information can be obtained
at www.ICGtesting.com
Printed in the USA
JSHW042337191021
19689JS00001B/32